8 MOTIVATING STORIES ON SELF-LOVE BECAUSE 'HAPPINESS IS NOT BY CHANCE, BUT BY CHOICE.'

PRERNA BHATNAGAR

BLUEROSE PUBLISHERS
India | U.K.

For permissions requests or inquiries regarding this publication, please contact:

BLUEROSE PUBLISHERS
www.BlueRoseONE.com
info@bluerosepublishers.com
+91 8882 898 898
+4407342408967

ISBN: 978-93-6452-668-5

First Edition: June 2024

About the Author

Prerna's debut book, 'I'm in Love with Me', achieved the status of #1 Amazon Bestseller and left a profound and lasting impression on its readers, sparking a meaningful dialogue on self-love and personal growth.

In 2024, Fox Story India honoured her as the 'Women Face of the Year' under the category of authors who made a positive impact on society.

Prerna has learned to embrace herself and find inner peace, instead of staying caught in other peoples' mini dramas. Now, she aims to bring inspiring anecdotes to life so that her readers can be empowered to contemplate their own obstacles, find inner peace, and elevate their overall well-being.

WOMEN

FACES OF THE YEAR 2024

CERTIFICATE

OF APPRECIATION TO

Prerna Bhatnagar

AMAZON #1 BESTSELLING AUTHOR

She is an indomitable spirit, filled with unwavering dedication and guided by passion, and has made her mark on the society. Her tireless pursuit for excellence fanned the flames of inspiration in many. It is with great pride and honor, Fox Story India presents the title.

MEDIA HEAD

"To my Guruji,

who has walked every step of this journey with me,

and

to my parents,

who have gifted me the power to live life with love,
faith, and kindness."

"You are what you believe yourself to be."

–Paulo Coelho

Preface

"I'm still in Love with Me" will pick your spirits further from "I'm in Love with Me". Moving and uplifting, this is an exhilarating collection of heartwarming anecdotes that will engross and motivate every reader.

This book chronicles the journeys of 8 inspiring individuals, men and women, who, like many of us, have faced their own share of challenges. Their stories, filled with resilience and determination, will resonate with readers, helping them realize the untapped power of their own will.

Make sure you read carefully, as these tales may hold clues to help you confidently answer the following life questions and discover the breakthrough that may shape your own happiness story.

- How does one find and protect their inner peace?
- How can one identify and take a stand in toxic situations and relationships?
- How does one stop saying "yes" when they mean to say a "no"?

- How can one find freedom from people and situations that own them?
- How does one understand their inner calling and unleash their passion?

Life is too short to spend another day at war with ourselves. If our current situation looks awful, we may wish to go back and change the beginning. However, can't we start where we are and change the ending?

Introduction

I'm a woman in my happy 40s, an age where I have few wrinkles and some grey hair too. As I look at the more youthful women with beauty and zest, I reminisce about my younger self.

The Twenties -

The early 20s were marked by experimentation, chaos, trial and error!

Everyone seemed older and more respected.

While I was struggling to find my life path, they all seemed to 'have their plans together'.

As I grew more independent and mobile, I made many new friends.

By my mid-20s, I had dived headfirst into my career, got married, and had my first child.

The Thirties -

Career pinnacled as I had the skills to meet my intentions.

I met some fascinating people but lost touch with many dear friends.

I was a better employee, a wiser mother (of two), a more responsible daughter and a better spouse.

The Forties -

I feel classy, like a vintage car or a fine wine.

The wisdom and experience I possess are priceless.

I dealt with the loss of a parent with courage.

Today I am raising kids, managing a career, and running the household well.

I have fewer new friends but have rekindled old friendships that had faded away in my 30s.

The best gift @40 - I holistically discovered self-love and became a published author!

As I excitedly embrace the process of ageing, I'm ready to blaze a new trail and become a pioneer in whatever makes me happy! We are often taught to "be kind to others" while growing up, but through my book, let me show you how to put another life mantra into practice: "*Be kind to yourself*"!

Contents

Story 1

My sweet truth!

Sugar is the world's love language!

Whether it is a child going for an exam with the customary dahi-cheeni, a relative bringing a mithai ka dabba with a wedding invitation, a Mundan ceremony, or even a Shradh ceremony after a funeral, our relationship with sugar stands strong in happy or sad times!

We can effortlessly recall a slice of cake at a celebration, cups of tea shared with loved ones, or a thoughtful box of chocolates we received as a farewell gift. Remember those heartwarming Cadbury advertisements that evoke nostalgia and make us all go "aww"? Its catchy slogan, "Kuch Meetha ho jaye," is etched in our hearts forever!

So, since sugar continues to serve as a meaningful and enduring expression of warmth and connection, the not-so-sweet truth is that our country is already the diabetes capital of the world, with a staggering 26% of people diagnosed in the diabetic or pre-diabetic range. If we think about undiagnosed diabetics, this figure may look even more alarming. It wouldn't be wrong to say that sugar is proving to be as toxic as tobacco these days!

Packaged foods are notorious for containing excessive hidden sugars. This has contributed to a significantly higher incidence of diabetes in urban India as compared to rural areas. Shockingly, this rise includes a significant percentage of children. The culprits behind this unsettling reality are indeed the concealed sugars found in products considered 'health drinks', ‘healthy breakfast cereals’, bread, biscuits, and ketchup.

It is a custom to make an Om mark with honey on the tongue of a newborn baby in India, and most of us have begun our love affair with sweet foods since then. My relationship with this staple ingredient was also hard to rewire as it was decades old.

Growing up, desserts were a significant part of our family tradition. My siblings and I were always excited about the homemade halwa and kheer that our parents would treat us to. As I entered my teenage years, I found myself developing a sweet tooth, often indulging in a little post-dinner treat. I used to rationalise it by thinking, "A little sweet indulgence won't hurt, right?"

Like most youngsters, I loved cupcakes, muffins, and cold coffee or shakes and rejoiced in ice cream dates with friends and family. I remember the times when relatives brought chocolates for me and my brother. If it was a big bar, I recollect licking my leftover chocolate before securing it back in the wrapping paper, announcing this act, and only then keeping it in the fridge as bhai won't eat 'jhootha khana'!

As time went by, I married Punit. Despite facing challenges in our jobs, we were both successful in our careers. I received promotions and awards, and I experienced steady professional growth.

When we found out about our first pregnancy, tests showed that I had gestational diabetes, which is a type of diabetes that can develop during pregnancy in women who did not have high sugar levels before conceiving. Both my father's and mother's sides of the family have a history of diabetes. However, it only manifested when they were around 55 years old, unlike me, because they were leading a highly active and healthy lifestyle.

At this point, I was advised to refrain from anything sweet. It was time to plan a family, and control was required. However, many evenings that I didn't indulge in a sweet treat, my mouth would water, and my stomach would growl and crave. I tried different tactics to break the spell, but nothing really stuck. Most days, I'd sneak a chocolate cookie here and there. So soon, doctors put me on insulin injections, and I started mentally beating myself up for my lack of discipline.

A few days after the birth of my daughter, Ourjaa, my blood sugar levels returned to normal. However, I was cautioned against consuming sugar, as women with gestational high blood sugar levels are at a higher risk of developing full-blown diabetes.

I, however, reflected on the excruciating pain of childbirth and how I endured all the challenges and thought of pampering myself for just a few days. The sad part was that, despite being fully aware of sugar's detrimental effects on my health, I found myself indulging in it and longing for more.

I frequently ate my daughter's high-calorie leftovers, such as sooji kheer, cerelac, and cheeni parantha (loaded with ghee). One side effect of parenting was also lack of sleep, and the way she wore my energies down, I usually felt a little sorry for myself. So, a few scoops of baby milk powder made everything better.

Five years ahead, we were blessed with our second baby, our little brat, Tanishque. This pregnancy was only slightly better than the first, as this time, again, I had gestational diabetes. However, I wasn't put on insulin.

Post-second delivery, I enjoyed the brisk weight loss as I continued to avoid extra sugar and carbs. Lactating also helped me get back in shape during my maternity leave. I loved the compliments that I received as I looked fitter and my skin glowed.

However, things slipped back as I re-joined work. The physical, emotional, and professional demands led to constant tiredness. Inadvertently, I again started reaching for carb-rich and sugary foods for a boost to balance irritability, emotional lows, and other stresses. Turning to chocolate or an innocent scoop of ice cream to comfort myself felt logical at that time.

Years went by, and I realised that I was not on any corporate ladder but on a gameboard of corporate 'Snakes & Ladders'. I climbed carefully up the steps to success; still, at several places, snakes lurked and bit, leaving me feeling frustrated and painful as I sledged back down.

I struggled to strike a balance between being a good mom and being a successful professional. My team and I literally slogged around the clock to meet deadlines, and most often, I caught myself working even while sleeping.

Despite this, it was challenging because top management was tough to please. Unlike most employees, who are overly enthusiastic and offer blind support to every command by the boss, I used my logic and reasoning. As a result, I often ended up feeling overwhelmed or contradicted.

I relied on sugar as a "quick fix" during every long and stressful day, and this vicious cycle continued for many years.

This picture is from my official trip to Kolkata, where I visited Mishti Hub, a one-stop shop for sweet lovers. Mishti Hub has a variety of shops providing both modern and traditional sweets from all over West Bengal. It may sound unbelievable, but I genuinely indulged in eight distinct varieties of sweets and relished three different-flavoured flavoured yoghurts for breakfast before embarking on my hectic day!

Here, let me pause and ask:

Do you also feel a sugar rush gushing through your veins when you are very stressed?

If yes, it's natural! Sugar releases endorphins in the body, which results in a surge of energy. However, once this energy boost has peaked, blood sugar levels drop abruptly, leading to lethargy, a low mood, and further cravings. So, before we realise it, we develop a sugar addiction!

Coming back to my story, on a comfortable Sunday morning, while sipping my morning tea and enjoying a chocolate cookie, I came across an intriguing newspaper column discussing the phenomenon of sugar addiction. As I delved into the article, a sudden realisation hit me.

I couldn't ignore the feeling that something was off and unsettling. This prompted me to retrieve the long-forgotten weighing scale from the cluttered corner of the storeroom. After dusting it off, I hesitantly stepped onto the scale and was taken aback by the number that flashed before me. It was a shocking revelation: I had reached my highest recorded weight, surpassing even the weight I had during my full-term pregnancy.

It wouldn't be an exaggeration to say that I went into an emotional coma and felt like a stranger in my own body. A series of diagnostic tests followed, and I was declared to be in the pre-diabetic range. The HBA1C and bad cholesterol count acted like a frightening wake-up call, and I felt flabbergasted.

Soon, on the recommendation of a few trusted colleagues, I reached out to Shikha, my dietician. Not only did she give me the confidence to turn things around, but she also made me appreciate the parameters on which I scored well in these diagnostic tests, like haemoglobin, calcium, etc.

Shikha came into my life like a North Star, lighting my way in the darkest of nights. Her guidance and support have truly been my guiding light, helping me navigate towards a path of improved health and happiness.

In September 2023, I took my first leap to reduce, if not eliminate, sugar from my diet. However, it was more difficult than I imagined, as I found myself experiencing withdrawal symptoms of irritability, glumness, and low energy. Until now, I had a sugar addiction where I was binging on sugary foods, so the withdrawal and cravings were intense.

Unfortunately, a significant number of individuals succumb to the temptation of consuming sugary foods as a result of the chemical reactions that occur in the brain. I, too, fight a frequent battle to resist this urge. Honestly, most days, I win, and some days, I lose. However, if I feel defeated by the lure of sugar consecutively for two instances, I try to remember the lousy feeling I had when I had just started in September, as the sugar lust lasts for a couple of minutes but the awful guilt lingers for a much longer duration. Thus, I now try to leave the sugary beverages on the grocery store's shelf, as these sugar-sweetened pick-me-ups have been my one-way ticket to high blood sugar. Eliminating or drinking them only occasionally has really helped.

Not completely, but at least for one meal a day, I have substituted wheat and rice with ragi. A variety of season-specific detox waters have also been a boon to reducing water retention. The mid-meal hunger pangs still attack, but I try to combat them with roasted foxnuts, seasonal fruits, and flavourful sprouted salads versus cookies, unhealthy snacks, and coffee. I have to remind myself to stay hydrated constantly.

In order to maintain a healthy lifestyle, I have adopted a balanced approach and allowed myself the indulgence of one or two treats a week, which are my 'cheat' moments. However, I don't punish myself if I slip a little with three or four sweet treats occasionally. So far, I have managed to lose approximately 8 kilograms, and my glucose levels are gradually returning to normal. I am making progress little by little, but consistently, in order to achieve a harmonious relationship with my body.

Through trial and error, I am learning a way that works for me. There is no place for self-criticism, as it has been replaced with self-love and compassion. Each day, I genuinely relish the progress I'm making towards a more positive and fulfilling life. After all, good health is a journey, not a destination!

Story 2

Superwoman in an Apron

Among the busiest and most diligent people are homemakers. They spend most of their time caring for the household and performing chores at home, never taking a day off. The beginning of Nita Uppal's journey also started as a homemaker.

In India, especially in villages and Tier II cities, women still depend on their fathers, husbands, or sons for financial or non-financial requirements. At Uppal Niwas, Nilesh Uppal, who worked at the State University as a head librarian, was the decision-maker. Nita, however, was indisputably the 'Queen of her Kitchen', and all ingredients seemed to obey her orders so she could create the most perfect dishes. Her recipes, like the rich and creamy Shahi Tukda or the aromatic Biryani, were the talk of the locality.

It's interesting to note that in Nita's neighbourhood, whenever someone made a special dessert or delicacy, they would send a tiffin full to Nita's home. This served two purposes: first, Nita could provide great insights on how the dish could be improved, and second, it is a common custom in India that an empty vessel is never returned without filling it with another food item. Therefore, any vessel returned from Nita's kitchen obviously contained something delicious, which everyone was eager to enjoy.

Food was more than just a source of nourishment for Nita. She truly believed it to be a celebration of life that fosters bonds between family and friends. Her feasts, the centre point of every festival in the modest locality, brought the community together in joy and celebration.

However, her twin sons, Raghu and Raghav, hated indulging in food. Instead of eating fresh, home-cooked meals, they preferred protein drinks, boiled egg whites, and boxed cornflakes. They kept telling their mother not to spend much time in the kitchen and thought the feasts their parents hosted were a complete waste of time, money, and effort.

Years passed, and the boys grew into charming young men in their early twenties. While Raghav moved to Delhi to work as an accountant for an enterprise, Raghu started getting ready for a career in modelling. In the interim, he took up a job as a personal trainer at his friend's gym.

As the boys took over the responsibility of their careers, Nilesh also decided to take a voluntary retirement. Amid all these changes, Nita, as usual, continued with her zest for cooking.

It was March 2020, and the Uppal duo had a merry time organising the Holi festivity get-together with a few other grey-haired couples in their social circle. In all these gatherings, news of the fast-spreading coronavirus was also discussed, though in low magnitude. The virus, however, spread well beyond its origins in China, wreaking havoc in India in less than fifteen days of Holi.

Soonest and least expected, in the late-evening address to the nation on March 24, 2020, Prime Minister Narendra Modi announced his plan to lock down India to combat the coronavirus outbreak.

Following the lockdown declaration, the country experienced the most significant mass movement of people since India's split in 1947. Raghav also came back to Gwalior to stay with his brother and parents. While the Corona outbreak was spreading like wildfire, Nita was overjoyed when the lockdown began.

During the lockdown, she could spend valuable time with her sons while the entire family was home. Interestingly, the once-neglected TV set, which had been no more than a mere decorative object in their living room, also regained its importance and became the centre of attention. The family binge-watched nostalgic serials like Ramanand Sagar's Ramayan, the epic Mahabharat series (by B. R. Chopra), and many others like Buniyaad and Shaktiman together. To the Uppal family, it was like revisiting the good old days, and no one thought much about the virus, almost convinced they would be safe.

After a few weeks, however, the truth of the situation began to dawn on them. The Government of India continued to extend the nationwide lockdown, and everyone felt trapped inside the house. The initial excitement of spending time together and revisiting old memories was replaced by a sense of restlessness and anxiety. The Uppal family, like many others, was grappling with the emotional toll of the pandemic.

Nita missed spending time with her friends, having meals together, and going for evening walks. Her friends also missed enjoying the delicious food she used to cook. They now stayed connected through mobile phones and celebrated events like birthdays and anniversaries through Zoom parties.

Nilesh, Raghu, and Raghav also grappled with the effects of the current situation. In the absence of any social interaction and uncertainty, they actively sought ways to maintain a positive outlook and stay optimistic.

Although Nilesh continued to receive his pension, Raghav experienced a setback as his salary was withheld, and he was placed on unpaid leave. Raghu, on the other hand, struggled to find a stable source of income as his modelling career was put on hold due to the pandemic, and his attempts at online Zumba sessions encountered a lack of response from potential participants.

It was the first time in the prosperous Uppal Niwas that there was a wave of disappointment, and the novelty of being at home quickly wore off.

If financial uncertainty wasn't enough, there was news of close relatives and friends falling prey to COVID-19. The constant fear and worry about the health and safety of their loved ones added to the emotional burden on the Uppal family, making it even more difficult to cope with the situation.

Late one evening in May, the Uppal family was awakened by a distress call at 11 PM from their neighbours, the Deshpandes, who lived in the same housing society. The elderly couple, their son, daughter-in-law, and four-year-old granddaughter were all affected. They were struggling to prepare an essential meal and pleaded for help as their granddaughter wailed with hunger. Nilesh and Nita loved playing with the little girl. Her screams today, however, shook them from within.

Thankfully, Nita had boiled potatoes to prepare bread rolls for breakfast the following day. So, she quickly prepared some stuffed paranthas, packed them in a disposable box, and left the food at their doorstep.

For the next few days, she delivered food to Deshpandes until the family recovered. By the end of the next week, Mr. Deshpande posted a thank-you note for Nita in the residents' WhatsApp group. On the same day, she received three more requests for food delivery from sick neighbouring families.

Meanwhile, the Deshpandes sent Rs. 2000 to the Uppals by online transfer as a token of gratitude and requested that they start a meal service for suffering residents. Initially reluctant, Nilesh and Nita saw merit in this much-needed service and agreed.

Nita's dal, sabzi, chapati, and rice now filled stomachs and hearts, too. People widely appreciated her efforts, and a lady known for the aroma of her food gained popularity for her kindness, unity, and support for the community. In just a month, Nita served over twenty families in and around the neighbourhood.

She kept a simple and nutritious menu and charged a nominal fee of Rs. 50 for breakfast and Rs. 100 for lunch or dinner for two. Raghu, on his bike, delivered these meals to people's doorsteps while complying with COVID protocols and covering a radius of up to 5 km.

From a homemaker to a successful homepreneur, Nita's journey soon became a testament to the power of determination and passion. A local NGO recognised her contribution, and she started receiving orders for over 75 meals a day.

Soon, Nita's quaint backyard transformed into a bustling mini-catering unit. She, along with her dedicated assistant cooks and delivery team, consisting of Nilesh, Raghav, and Raghu, orchestrated a seamless operation that brought her vision to life. This remarkable transformation not only revolutionised Nita's daily routine but also inspired everyone around her, demonstrating the remarkable possibilities that can be achieved with dedication and the right mindset to overcome adversity.

During the second wave of COVID-19, Nita's remarkable resilience and ability to adapt inspired many, as she played a significant role in helping people navigate difficult times. She expanded her services from COVID-19-positive, home-bound patients to families observing the tradition of not cooking for thirteen days post-death and also frontline healthcare workers. Supported by three dedicated domestic helpers, she successfully met the high demand, showcasing her ability to thrive in challenging circumstances.

People often address Nita Uppal as Annapurna (the goddess of food and nourishment), and today, even after the deadly pandemic, her day starts at 6:30 AM. She has a network of home-based cooks and now supplies fresh, nutritious meals to nearby nursing homes and hostels. While Raghav resumed his accountancy career in Delhi, Raghu and Nilesh joined Nita wholeheartedly in her mission.

She is steadfast and defies several typecasts to pursue her passion with zeal. All her dishes still have dollops of taste and nutrition; the only difference is that she cooks now as a homemaker and as a homepreneur. Her enthusiasm is getting in top gear as she plans to apply for an FSSAI licence (Food Safety and Standards Authority of India) to register her kitchen commercially.

Indeed, Nita's genuine inclination to cook and serve continues to transform her life by leaps and bounds. Raghu and Raghav had always loved their mother, but now they have deep respect and admiration for her as she proved to be Annapurna for their family and several others.

Story 3

Faith is stronger than fear

Debasree fondly reminisces about her enchanting childhood in a picturesque small town near Jamshedpur. Everything seemed unusually enchanting in those days; the trees stood tall and grand, the colours seemed exceptionally vibrant, and each new day brought a thrilling promise, surpassing the excitement of the one before.

She spent numerous years immersed in studies at the hostel, but despite this, Debasree maintained a solid and intimate bond with her parents, having been raised as the only child.

After graduating with a degree in Physics Hons., she made an unconventional choice by pursuing a Diploma in Travel and Tourism and an IATA course. Despite the unconventional nature of her decision, it proved to be transformative.

Not long after, an exciting opportunity arose for Debasree to join the esteemed British Airways, where she managed ticketing, check-in, load controls, and reservations. Her remarkable intellect and ambition were quickly recognised as she effortlessly cleared internal assessments within a mere fortnight of joining the company. This accomplishment led to her selection for special training in Delhi, marking only the initial step in her illustrious professional journey.

Over the next six months, Debasree experienced a career opportunity beyond her wildest dreams when she was flown to the United Kingdom by British Airways. Based in London, she explored various parts of Europe, such as Hamburg, Switzerland, Italy, and France, and even ventured through a significant portion of Canada.

As a young woman in her early twenties, the experience of being exposed to a global setting was incredibly impactful. She had the opportunity to study aviation under the guidance of a skilled Danish mentor and collaborated with a diverse multinational team consisting of individuals from British, Kenyan, and Indian backgrounds.

In the midst of the airline's continued expansion in Kuwait and Muscat, Debasree found herself embracing a heightened level of global exposure. However, as her professional life reached new heights, she also felt the pull to focus on her personal life. In 2001, Debasree and Shekar celebrated their love in a heartfelt and intimate wedding ceremony, marking the beginning of a new chapter in their lives.

Shekar and Debasree were a fantastic couple from two different corners of India. Debasree, a Bengali, and Shekar, a Tamilian, had a beautiful love that effortlessly transcended their diverse cultural backgrounds. Their incredible journey took them around the world, hand in hand, from the charming streets of Vancouver to the bustling city of San Francisco, delighting their friends and family.

In 2002, life became even more joyful when they welcomed their beautiful daughter, Anushka.

The next few years were marked by some challenges, including the heartbreak of a miscarriage and the arduous task of managing their daughter, along with careers in different cities, one in Kolkata and the other in Delhi. However, time stood still, and blissful tears rolled down their cheeks as they held their son Satya in their arms in 2008.

Life was hectic with two young children and a demanding profession. However, it was also a time of spiritual awakening for Debasree. In 2014, a close friend encouraged her to explore Buddhism through Soka Gakkai International (SGI). As a newcomer, she actively participated in member meetings and gradually developed a profound connection to the teachings, finding them enlightening. Specifically, chanting the Lotus Sutra (Nam-myoho-renge-kyo) significantly impacted her, lifting her spirits and instilling the ability to perceive challenges as opportunities through unwavering faith and self-belief.

Over the course of 18 years, Debasree dedicated herself to her career. Her practice of Buddhism gave her the inner strength to confront her insecurities, and she decided to take a hiatus from work to focus on her personal life. This period of self-reflection and growth also coincided with the loss of her father, a deeply challenging time in her life. Drawing from Soka Gakkai International's (SGI) principles, Debasree found the fortitude to navigate this profound loss. Through it all, she was also preparing for the trials and triumphs that awaited her.

In 2016, Shekar and Debasree visited a dental clinic for a minor tooth issue. While waiting at the reception, Shekar noticed a brochure about health checkups. They realised that they hadn't undergone any tests in years, so they decided to schedule a comprehensive full-body checkup.

Debasree's world turned upside down upon receiving the distressing news after her ultrasound appointment. The suspicion of breast cancer shook her to the core, and a biopsy was required to clarify the diagnosis. With her husband, Shekar, away in Chennai, without even informing him, she faced the daunting biopsy by herself.

The biopsy results arrived without delay, confirming Debasree's worst fears. The doctors' sombre expressions and carefully chosen words delivered the crushing blow of a cancer diagnosis. When Shekar learned of her condition, disbelief and devastation consumed him at the thought of losing his beloved wife.

However, Debasree's unwavering faith and determination stood as a sharp sword, ready to confront and overcome any darkness or negativity that lay ahead. She dauntlessly went through chemotherapy for four months and was slated for surgery to remove part of her breast and a few lymph nodes after that.

During her chemotherapy sessions, Debasree found solace in chanting the Lotus Sutra. Knowing that chemotherapy can harm healthy cells along with cancerous ones, she turned to the calming words of the sutra to help reduce the adverse effects of the treatment. She recited the sutra with deep faith with each session, feeling stronger and more resilient.

After about 2–3 weeks of chemotherapy, her hair loss started. Hair loss, or alopecia, may make patients feel vulnerable, self-conscious, and exposed to the world as "cancer patients." Many also take it as a trigger for the heightened anger and depression that cancer may cause. But Debasree embraced this situation bravely.

She proactively decided to shave off her hair before the surgery.

Yes, looking in the mirror and not recognising herself initially was disorienting. However, Debasree decided to celebrate the person within and focus on beautifying her inner self.

She found her new style statement in scarves of many styles and colours. The primary idea was not to hide her hair loss but to feel well-groomed and protect her scalp from the sun. Her friends from all over the country and the world contributed to this enthusiastic addition to her wardrobe, and she soon had a huge fashionista-like collection of scarves matching each outfit and occasion.

As Debasree fought, life became more challenging, and finances evaporated rapidly. Six days a week and for three weeks, doctors put her on radiation therapy. She was also placed on uber-expensive hormone injections, which dried up most of the family's savings. But God helps those who keep faith and remain fearless, no matter what. Thus, Debasree got timely assistance from her treating doctor, who connected her to a distributor to reduce her medical expenses significantly.

The diagnosis of Debasree's cancer impacted the lives of the entire family. Their daily routine, activities, and expenses all required coping approaches that varied with different phases of the treatment. Life, however, was slowly coming back to normalcy.

It was June 10th, 2017, Debasree and Sekhar's wedding anniversary. The couple enjoyed a hearty lunch as their marital bond attained a 'Sweet 16 badge' that day. The kids were at their grandmother's home in Kolkata for their summer vacations, so the duo spent quality time in each other's company throughout the day. In the evening, the kids brought to life sweet memories from the family album and bombarded their parents' smartphones with nostalgia. "What a beautiful anniversary celebration!" the couple thought as they retired for the evening.

Some moments stay in our memory for a long time, and a few are itched in our hearts forever. This anniversary celebration belonged to the latter, as life changed entirely for the family after that.

On June 11th, Sekhar woke up as usual at 6:30 AM and performed his Surya Namaskar. As he proceeded towards the washroom, Debasree lazed in bed for a little longer. While half asleep, she heard a huge thud and ran towards the bathroom to find Sekhar on the floor!

Sekhar had a robust body, so Debasree rushed to get help from the neighbours. They could gauge that something was wrong and wasted no time giving him a mouth-to-mouth Cardiopulmonary resuscitation (CPR), which could be lifesaving in many emergencies when someone's breathing or heartbeat is erratic. Sekhar, however, was not responding.

Debasree was taken aback by the realisation that Sekhar had passed away, even though the doctors had not yet officially confirmed it. As the medical verification process unfolded and the family rushed to the hospital, she found herself struggling to come to terms with how life could change so dramatically within just a few hours.

Days later, as she reflected on the memories of the warm and affectionate life she had shared with her late husband, the overwhelming sense of loss and the daunting prospect of single-handedly taking care of the family weighed heavily on her mind. Without a source of income and her children still in school, she found herself at rock bottom. However, amidst the darkness, she discovered a reservoir of inner strength and made a conscious decision to shield herself from succumbing to grief. She was determined to overcome every challenge and refused to entertain the thought of giving in to despair.

When facing adversity, we may think we've reached our limit, but the darker the night, the nearer the dawn. So, Debasree started her rigorous job search despite her treatment and emotional hardships. Throughout this struggle, she realised that the true secret of success is the refusal to give up, and the risk of failure is only part of trying. Thus, she vowed never to give up, and her self-belief was rewarded by a reputed job at IndiGo Airlines in October 2017.

Anushka and Satya were too young to come to terms with their father's death. But the reality is harsh and, most of the time, cruel and ugly. Yet, nothing changes, no matter how much we grieve over our circumstances. So, she taught them to understand the importance of not feeling defeated and to forge ahead bravely so newer paths could open before them.

This proved accurate, as Anushka scored 92% on her 10th-grade boards despite all odds. She even made it to the Brown Ivy School in the USA for her summer exposure. Now a triple major in British English, psychology, and media, she is making her mother proud with her accomplishments at a renowned PR and marketing firm. Although still in school, Satya is also doing well in his studies and aspires to fulfil his parents' dream.

Notably, Debasree's struggles augmented during the prime COVID era, despite her supportive and firm professional standing. In March 2020, when the nation was adjusting to the lockdown, Debasree was told about a black spot in her ribs, which grew more prominent in 2021. Only three weeks after her college enrollment, Anushka was made to travel back to sign her mother's surgery consent letter, and Debasree's cancerous 8th posterior rib was removed!

Keeping all ailments aside, our lives as humans are indeed extraordinary. One may be physically ill, but if our mental health is robust, it most certainly exerts a positive influence on the body. In Debasree's case, too, there hasn't been a better medicine than faith. Month after month, she boldly takes painful bone-strengthening injections and confidently manages her physically and financially demanding cancer treatment.

Debasree is a true inspiration and a beacon of hope for many struggling with cancer and grief of any kind. She quotes what Buddhism taught her–that even a stone from the bottom of a river can produce fire. No matter how dark, our present sufferings have not continued for billions of years, nor will they linger forever. The sun will rise, and if it's pitch dark, believe its ascent has already begun.

Today, her conviction that **"If one lights a fire for others, one will brighten one's way too"** motivates her to guide her personal and professional community on cancer therapy, lifestyle modulation, and more. Debasree also undertakes many social initiatives, like helping the grassroots-level ground staff at the airport learn working English, finish their education, and apply for higher jobs.

Debasree's radiant smile and vibrant personality have triumphed over negativity, and her charisma rekindles hope and positivity. Her story serves as a powerful testament to the cycle of life—no matter how prolonged the dark and desolate winter may seem, spring will inevitably make its return!

Story 4

Angrezi Fever

When Bhimsen Tripathi and his newlywed wife, Rupa, first arrived in Mumbai from Varanasi, they were confronted by the harsh realities of their new life. Days turned into nights with empty stomachs, a stark contrast to the life they had left behind in their small town.

As time passed, Bhimsen found employment as a driver, enabling Rupa to stay home and care for their twin daughters. They secured a modest 10x10 room in a traditional Mumbai chawl but struggled to afford basic amenities like running water and electricity.

Over time, as the girls grew, Rupa also took on the role of a domestic worker to meet their educational expenses. Despite attending a Marathi Medium school, the couple was delighted that their daughters received instruction in basic English. The girls dedicated themselves to studying under streetlights or at a neighbours' kholi during exam times, and their hard work paid off with commendable grades, particularly in English.

Witnessing their daughters' dedication and success further fuelled the Tripathi couple's determination to provide their children with the opportunity for the finest education available. Bhimsen drove the district judge's car during the day and worked as a cleaner at a local food joint in the evenings. He and his wife saved money, and with Judge Sahib's help, they put both girls in an English-medium school (under the Economically Weaker Section quota) when they were in Grade 2.

After years of hard work and sacrifice, Bhimsen's determination led to the opening of a small grocery store. The shop flourished, and within a short span of two years, he was able to expand by acquiring an adjacent store. However, with the expansion came the need for more extensive, detailed inventory management, which meant long hours at the shop for Bhimsen and his wife. Their home became a brief respite only for recharging before plunging back into work, a testament to their unwavering commitment to their business and family.

The Tripathi couple had attended modest regional schools, with Rupa a seventh-grade pass and Bhimsen an intermediate certificate holder. However, despite limited formal education, they were street-smart and maintained systematic accounting practices at their store. Thus, their business kept expanding at a fast pace. Now, their daughters Mala and Deepa went to a convent school, where the dress code was Western, and the primary language of interaction was English.

Bhimsen had always worked industriously to provide his family with a comfortable life. He felt a sense of achievement when he compared their economic status with others who migrated with them. Mala and Deepa, however, felt embarrassed to introduce their parents to anyone.

They dreaded the PTM, which was organised once every quarter and wanted their parents to exit the school premises with minimal interaction. To the young daughters, being good at English meant being smart, and the older Tripathis couldn't manage it. Yes, senior Tripathis had a brush with the language at school, but their teacher himself could not speak English, and they all apparently studied even English in Hindi!!

Until the girls were in primary school, Bhimsen and Rupa did not pay much attention. However, as the daughters entered middle school, their parents started facing their stooping attitude. They avoided introducing their parents to friends and never invited anyone home. However, what was most disturbing was that the teenage sisters belittled them by cracking nasty jokes and passing daily sarcasm.

Mala and Deepa had access to resources beyond their parents' imagination. However, instead of feeling thankful, they felt ashamed. They left no chance to pick up on their parents' inability to communicate in the global lingua franca.

The Tripathi pair experienced a sense of unworthiness and discomfort as the girls created a hostile atmosphere in their own home. This made them feel unwelcomed and out of place, despite home being a space where one should feel the most at ease.

The lane in front of their house had a plethora of signboards of smart-looking, white-skinned professionals talking into a headset and glorifying English-speaking ability. Looking at these, both frequently pondered how a foreign language could capture the hearts and minds of the youth while Hindi is the Rashtra Bhasha of Bharat! What they also wondered is why millions of Indians accepted this. Is it simply because the young and the modern prefer English?

A language that never bothered them for several years in Mumbai started shattering their confidence now. Ridiculed at home, they suddenly felt incapable of understanding paperwork, tax forms, etc., without assistance, as most of it was in English.

They considered joining an English-speaking class for a while, hoping it would help them gain respect from their daughters and feel more confident. However, they quickly reversed their decision upon realizing the extent of their influence over Mala and Deepa's thoughts and actions.

Like all other Indian parents, they also aspired to enrol their children in a top English school. Bhimsen recalled that they had switched from an English medium school to another top International Baccalaureate (IB Board) school not too long back, where he paid a hefty bribe as they needed help to clear the parents' round, which was in English. So, no wonder, with such Angrezi madness they displayed, their daughters, like several other youngsters, now believed that their nation's prosperity, as well as their own, is wholly dependent upon learning English and exclusively using it as a first language.

The kids had zapped their emotional well-being to near zero for a while. Life seemed blurry to them, but upon reflecting on their journey and accomplishments in Mumbai, they began to restore their faith in themselves. This newfound self-belief was like a pair of 3D glasses at the movies, as everything looked sharp and bright to them!

They understood that throughout humanity's history, discrimination has existed in many forms, such as caste, creed, gender, nationality, race, and language. People have used various means to justify their superiority over others, but those who stand undeterred always stand as winners. Thus, they were now unaffected by sarcasm at home. Yes, it still felt terrible, but not strong enough to shake their self-esteem.

Time took a flight, and both daughters went to different cities to pursue higher education. The girls were relieved they would not face the daily cultural cringe as their parents would be in a different town.

Meanwhile, Tripathi seniors were busy operating their grocery business. They recently extended their customer offering by keeping pooja samagri (important items for doing holy rituals) at their store. This turned out to be a wise business decision because the majority of our population is religious, and people observe some ritual almost every other day.

Also, undoubtedly, for any happy or sad event, Pooja is mandatory; thus, they started with the most common pooja items, including incense sticks, coconuts, camphor, and sacred threads, and gradually scaled up to selling divine gifts items like deity idols, pooja thali sets with minakari work, and decorative brass diyas etc.

Mumbai is home to many nuclear families who do not have elderly parents or grandparents to guide them when organising a pooja; most feel lost when shopping for necessary pooja essentials. In this scenario, Rupa and Bhimsen brought a sense of respite. As Brahmins, they smartly utilised their religious expertise for suggestive selling and upselling their products.

For money-related success, they suggested items for Kubera Pooja or Dhanalakshmi Pooja. For family peace, items for Nav Graha Shanti (nine planets) would be sold. Saraswati Puja items were recommended for kids about to begin school. Likewise, for other reasons/occasions, their customised style worked very well.

Profits poured in, and soon, the couple secured leads for corporate gifting for the upcoming Diwali. Their meticulous preparations for the five-day festivity began in September, resulting in the sale of over 2,000 gift kits in their first year through word-of-mouth references!

A business referral also introduced them to a B2B company, which engaged Tripathis to supply pooja kits for distribution to the US, Canada, and Singapore. The couple introduced the Deepawali kit as their initial offering and later expanded their range to include kits for various occasions such as welcoming a new car, housewarming (griha pravesh), Holi, Ganapati Mahotsav, Durga puja, and more.

A typical puja kit contained 5–15 non-perishable items and instructions in Hindi and English to help facilitate the puja. The Indian population in these foreign countries embraced these kits wholeheartedly, leading to a remarkable 120% annual export growth. Within just two years, these exports accounted for a third of the company's total sales.

Mala and Deepa were pleasantly surprised when their friends excitedly informed them they had seen their parents' merchandise in several Walmart stores across the United States. Both daughters had worked hard to establish themselves in their respective careers and earned a comfortable income. However, they were astonished to learn that their parents, Bhimsen and Rupa, were bringing in more money in a month than their combined annual salaries. It was an unexpected turn of events for the sisters. The same parents who had embarrassed them since childhood had become a source of immense pride and admiration in just a few years.

The Tripathis adored their daughters, but unlike before, their children's affection, hate, pride, and prejudice did not diminish the self-love they had developed. Gone were the days when English tormented them as they communicated gracefully with their business counterparts in Hindi. The pair couldn't help but chuckle as they watched their English-speaking vendors make an effort to learn simple Hindi phrases to communicate more effectively with them.

After their inspirational professional feat, the couple now spends a happy retired life in their native village. They look back to the days when they hoped to learn English and earn acceptance and basic respect from their daughters, and many like them. But today, they are glad they did not cling to that needless goal. Instead, they disengaged from the suffering of holding on to false expectations.

The extraordinary tale of Bhimsen and Rupa Tripathi is a powerful reminder that sometimes in life, it's crucial to recognise the battles we're not meant to fight and the closed doors we're meant to let go of. By doing so, we create space for new opportunities to unfold. True contentment and purpose come when we embrace life as it is and redirect our path towards a more meaningful and fulfilling destination.

Story 5

Fat Debunked

Growing up, a lot of people experience body shaming, and for others, it can happen later in life, such as in middle age or after having children. Unfortunately, it can follow us everywhere, from schools and workplaces to family gatherings, friend circles, and even on social media.

Munmun Gandhi recalls the distressing experiences and mental struggles she endured because of being stigmatised and labelled a 'fat child'.

Until she turned ten, her relationship with food was one of pure joy. She would eagerly await her grandmother's freshly made aloo paranthas, savouring the rich flavours and the comforting warmth of the butter melting on top. During the particularly nerve-wracking math and science exam days, her mother packed Kesar Halwa with Pooris in her lunchbox, and its sweet, saffron-infused aroma immediately lifted her spirits, giving her the encouragement she needed to face the day.

Life was going well, and she enjoyed being called "cute-n-chubby" or "teddy-like" until she realised that these terms were used by people to body shame her.

"Your arms are too heavy."

"Your thighs are a little too flabby."

"Are you sure you want to wear that dress?"

"Try eating less, and you will be fine, beta."

"You are getting very chubby (read fat), beta."

"Try drinking lemon and honey in warm water on an empty stomach in the morning."

"Why don't you run and cycle for half an hour every morning and evening?"

"We were much fitter when we were your age."

These types of remarks and suggestions started even before she hit puberty, and they only began to increase as she got older. Until this time, even though her daadi and parents called it 'baby fat', her friends and classmates started addressing her as 'motu', 'elephant' and 'Tuntun Munmun'. School became a living hell, and fat-shaming seemed to be the norm, not only among students but also among teachers, who took pleasure in taunting kids about their physical appearance. Surprisingly, her thinner friends also began to be shamed of their weight and were told that they could blow away with the wind.

Munmun hit adolescence earlier than most of her friends. Everyone felt she looked more mature for her age, and the way her body grew made her hate her body even more. She started opting for dark-coloured clothes and wore a longer skirt at school. Munmun also ensured her shirts were loose so her torso wouldn't show.

It wasn't just people around her who were policing her diet. Magazines, advertisements, TV shows, movies, and social media exerted tremendous pressure. 'Fat' characters were often criticised and used for comic relief. As a result, Munmun began to feel submissive, and she would often cry in isolation, desperately wanting to change her entire body due to the hate it received not only from others but also from herself.

Munmun spent her free time watching weight loss videos and became obsessed with buying chia seeds, fat loss powders, etc., using her pocket money. During this time, she avoided looking in the mirror and never considered buying new clothes or accessories, even for special occasions. She also began excusing herself from most social functions and family gatherings.

She fantasized every night about having a thigh gap, a toned stomach, and well-defined arms and legs. Often, she pondered when she would attain the ideal physique she yearned for, especially in the eyes of her friends and family.

On her 16th birthday, she persuaded her mother to pay for a three-month gym subscription. She obsessively weighed herself before and after meals and often adjusted her posture, hoping to see a lower number on the scale. While she did lose some weight, she still felt that her overall body shape was too large for a teenager. Despite intense workouts, she remained dissatisfied with her stomach not being "flat" enough and felt that her body was never "good enough." This demotivated Munmun and made her feel even more disgusted with her body.

She began meticulously counting calories and restricting her meals to the point where she would often give her lunch to her friends and fill up on water. Unsurprisingly, one morning, she collapsed on the treadmill, sustaining a severe leg injury. Bedridden for nearly a week, she was strictly advised against exercising for several weeks. Despite this, Munmun's main concern was the fear of gaining weight, so she compensated by eliminating carbohydrates from her diet.

After several days of avoiding carbohydrates and not getting essential nutrients, her immune system became weak, and she had to be hospitalised. She stayed in the hospital for a week, and when she came home, she had severe swelling, dark circles around her eyes, and deficient energy levels. She was so weak that she couldn't even walk without help.

Munmun was confined to her bed for several weeks. This time she couldn't help but notice the deep concern etched onto her parents' faces and the frequent tears streaming down her grandmother's cheeks as they witnessed her deteriorating condition. It forced her to ponder whether all the extreme measures she had taken to lose weight were actually worth it.

Amidst societal pressure and striving to reach weight goals, she realised she had forgotten to respect her body. She understood that our bodies are not just for appearance but are meant to keep us alive and moving. Therefore, a number on the weighing scale cannot determine our worth.

Munmun realised that altering her physical appearance would not bring her true happiness; instead, learning to love and accept herself was the key. That particular day marked the beginning of her lifelong journey to self-love, during which she made peace with her body and embraced a newfound sense of harmony within herself.

After deciding to prioritise her recovery, Munmun consciously chose to seek out expert medical advice. She scheduled a consultation with a well-respected physician and underwent a series of thorough diagnostic tests.

In the consultation, the doctor stressed the importance of not relying solely on weight and body size to measure health. He emphasised the significance of considering a person's body composition, especially muscle mass. He explained that individuals with larger body frames could be healthier than their leaner counterparts, debunking the misconception that body size alone determines health. Furthermore, he discussed the complex role of genetics and its impact on body structure, highlighting the various factors that contribute to overall health.

In the meantime, Munmun's tests revealed that her sugar, cholesterol, thyroid, and all other measures were normal. She expressed her gratitude to the divine and resolved to embrace a healthy, balanced lifestyle from that moment onward.

Munmun's experience with illness and recovery over the past few months made her realise that she had been overly focused on being thin for many years. She understood that this pursuit had overshadowed the development of other essential aspects of her life.

While it's important to maintain a healthy weight, Munmun realised that this should not come at the expense of neglecting other areas of her well-being and personal growth. This marked a paradigm shift in her story as she now strives to be healthier, not just skinnier!

Today, Munmun confidently embraces her larger body size as she carries herself with grace and elegance to the pinnacle of the corporate ladder. Her free and flamboyant dressing style is unique, whether it's a 6-yard sari, a business suit, or a trendy salwar kameez. Upon achieving any professional milestone, she giggles, remembering her teenage years when she thought her weight would prevent her from succeeding in her career.

While reading Munmun's story, I'm sure many of you recalled your struggles with sadness, disappointment, and anger due to our society's obsession with unrealistic body standards. What can we expect when even the miracle of childbirth cannot shield a woman from the judgment and body shaming that follows post-pregnancy?

Remember that there will always be a beauty standard to which we don't fit, no matter how hard we try. So, instead of trying to fit in and seeking praise from others, let us try to keep ourselves happy.

Before concluding, I urge the readers to note their thoughts and acknowledge their own biases or judgments of others. So, the next time you're inclined to remark on a person's features, hair, complexion, or size, stop! Instead, consider it an opportunity to identify a favourable physical or non-physical trait and complement it appropriately. E.g. "you have a great smile" or "your handwriting is superb."

Let's commit to embracing our imperfections and those of everyone around us. Instead of dwelling on negativity, let's cultivate positive thoughts and affirmations to create a more beautiful, enriching life for all.

Story 6

Nightingale in a veil

Girija Devi was a young girl with a radiant face, full of innocence and energy. In accordance with the customs of her community, she entered into marriage at the tender age of four.

As per tradition, young girls like Girija were expected to stay in their parents's home until the "Gauna ceremony," a significant event that usually occurs after the child bride reaches puberty. Consequently, Girija continued to live with her parents while waiting for the symbolic transition to her husband's household.

As a young girl growing up in Rajasthan, Devi's father, Lotan Singh, exposed her to the rich world of folk music. He was a talented folk artist who entertained tourists with his soulful performances. From the moment Girija took her first steps, she eagerly joined him on stage, developing a deep passion for music. She was inspired by her father's artistic talents and felt a deep and irresistible longing to immerse herself in music and absorb his wealth of knowledge.

Girija possessed an electrifying energy in her voice that would unfailingly captivate her audience. Her singing exuded a profound depth that quickly garnered her widespread popularity. Soon, tour guides began clamouring to secure her performances for both domestic and international audiences. Breaking through language and cultural barriers, tourists from the USA, Europe, and Japan eagerly paid a generous fee to revel in her folk music performances set against the backdrop of vast sand dunes, camel caravans, and enchanting tales of royalty.

Lotan and his family lived in a small mud cottage for many years. To reach the house shared by Lotan's mother, wife, and three children, one had to make their way past a few cows and camels. The cottage had a wooden bed that occupied the entire space, leaving just enough room for two people to stand. Outside, the front yard had a charpai that was used for sleeping, eating, lounging, gossiping, and practising vocal music.

Over the next two to three years, as Girija's popularity grew, Lotan and his wife Bansi renovated their cottage into a cemented structure. They replaced the thatched roof with an asbestos ceiling and added a small toilet so no one had to step out to answer nature's call.

In the months that followed, the family used her earnings to buy a colour television and a table fan. They were also able to save enough money to cover the expenses for Girija's upcoming wedding functions. They felt glad about her achievements. However, their extended family and neighbours couldn't help but envy her success.

The tale of how Girija's in-laws discovered her singing talent is as fascinating as her mesmerizing voice. Girija's father-in-law, Bhawani Singh, a livestock trader, and her husband, Hari, were at the Pushkar fair for business purposes. The Pushkar fair, which has been held for over a hundred years, is not only a significant commercial event but also a vibrant showcase of Rajasthan's rich culture. Talented performers, including magicians, dancers, and snake charmers, gather at the fair to display their remarkable skills.

During the Pushkar Mela on a crisp November evening, Girija, adorned with a traditional 'ghoonghat' covering her head, took to the stage, holding a microphone with a sense of grace and poise. A diverse crowd, including many foreign tourists, gathered to witness the enchanting performance of this young girl in a predominantly male-dominated setting. As she commenced her devotional song, her melodic voice filled the air, evoking deep emotions and moving the audience to tears despite the language barrier. For Girija, it felt as though she was a liberated nightingale, soaring through the endless skies in her veil.

As the final notes of her performance echoed, the crowd erupted into thunderous applause. Girija's father beamed with pride and excitement as he hurried to greet her, only to be halted by her father-in-law, Bhawani Singh, who wore a pained expression.

Throughout Rajasthan, there exists a prevailing cultural taboo against female performers. Bhawani Singh, like many others, held the belief that women who performed in public were to be equated with the courtesans who entertained in the majestic courts of the Maharajas in the past.

After several heated discussions and serious accusations, Bhawani called off the marriage. Despite Lotan's sincere attempts to persuade him, nothing worked. Eventually, even Girija's uncles decided to cut ties with the family, and the villagers started a boycott. The whole community agreed that Girija had brought shame upon them, with the general feeling being that girls should not go beyond certain boundaries.

The hurtful remarks from the villagers cut deep into Girija's heart, but her unyielding determination and passion for music propelled her forward. She vowed that the harsh criticism would only steel her resolve and fuel her determination to succeed.

Meanwhile, her mother, Bansi, started welling up in sorrow, often sobbing at the slightest mention of Girija's life ahead. While Girija's father, Lotan, was busy supporting his daughter's musical pursuits, there was no one to comfort Bansi. She soon became very ill, and the doctor at the village dispensary advised the family to seek treatment in the city, where better medical facilities were available.

Girija and her parents made the difficult decision to relocate to Jaipur for a temporary period to seek treatment. Everything about the new city was unfamiliar to them, from the way people interacted with each other to their attire and cultural beliefs. They settled into a one-room kholi in a bustling slum area, mentally preparing themselves to adapt to the noise and pace of urban life for the next two months. During this time, Bansi needed to undergo regular hospital visits and receive necessary medication, so their presence in Jaipur was crucial.

Girija, accustomed to the open spaces and fresh air of the village, often felt suffocated in the congested city surroundings. However, she knew that her mother's health was their top priority, so in order to support the family's expenses, she quickly secured a job as a labourer at a construction site. Though her musical aspirations lay dormant as she worked with bricks and mortar, she found satisfaction in knowing that her efforts were aiding in her mother's recovery.

One morning, Girija woke up to the sound of rainfall hitting the tin roof. As she opened her eyes, she could see the grey clouds in the sky, indicating that the monsoon had arrived in full force. It was only the beginning of July, and the slum dwellers already dreaded the brunt of the monsoon fury. Over the past few days, the rainwater had been gushing in through a crack in the corner of their kholis, making it challenging to keep the living space dry and comfortable during the incessant downpour. However, to Girija, the rains were a great respite from the scorching heat.

On that particular day, she felt an unexplained bliss as she breathed in the earthy aroma that filled the air. As she prepared the morning meal on her 'chulha' the rhythmic sound of the rain on the tin roof and the smell of wet mud outside filled her with a sense of peace and contentment that had been missing for a long time.

She couldn't help but sing sweetly, her melodic voice blending with the pitter-patter of raindrops, uplifting her spirits to match the dark, blue sky. The soothing tones of Rag Malhar, a traditional Indian raag associated with the monsoon season, resonated within her, further lighting up her mood and infusing her with a sense of joy and tranquility amidst the storm.

Incidentally, Rekha Rani, a famous philanthropist, was in the slum to provide relief measures to the poor residents from the havoc rains may cause. How could anyone fail to recognize a voice as unique as Girija's? So, yes, Rekha also unconsciously started moving towards it. For the first time in her life, she heard a folk voice that was so unique and refreshing that it literally transported her to the vast, sandy landscapes of Rajasthan.

On that particular day, Rekha's discovery set the stage for Girija's remarkable ascent to stardom. In just ten days, the talented folk artist had the opportunity to showcase her skills at the prestigious two-day festival hosted by the Sansktrutik Kala Manch and the Bharat Kala Academy. This incredible opportunity allowed her to connect with numerous men and women hailing from lesser-known villages and local communities, all of whom were using their unique talents to leave a lasting impact both within the country and beyond its borders.

In this unfamiliar and enchanting new realm, her music, deeply rooted in the local flavour, began to challenge the gender disparity she had encountered since childhood delicately. Subsequently, she got an opportunity to participate in a series of cultural events, including the celebrated Rajasthani Folk Festival, Jaipur Arts Festival, and many more.

Today, Girija is playing a significant role in driving positive changes within her community. In addition to excelling in her musical pursuits, she has taken on the responsibility of mentoring and empowering over 50 women from her community who are interested in folk music. Her dedication and efforts are making a meaningful impact on the lives of these women and the cultural fabric of the community as a whole.

Interestingly, Hari, who had been engaged to Girija in their childhood, managed to locate her and decided to support her musical journey as her life partner. Today, Hari not only accompanies Girija on her musical tours but also continues to share the stage with her, showcasing his skills on the sarangi as they perform together.

India is a nation with a rich cultural tapestry, a dynamic contemporary presence, and a future brimming with potential. It is home to a myriad of talented individuals whose expertise spans various domains such as art, culture, music, business, politics, science, technology, philosophy, and sports. In the realm of music, India has been a cradle for remarkable singers whose contributions have left an indelible mark on the landscape of both Indian and global music.

As the rich and diverse musical tradition of our nation continues to shape and influence the world in profound ways, individuals like Girija, who possess remarkable courage and stand up for their beliefs, play a pivotal role in upholding the nation's pride and cultural heritage.

Story 7

Happiness blooms like flowers!

Vardaan Goel was a charming young boy who blossomed in the affectionate embrace of his household. His father owned a small electrical shop, offering basic electrical provisions and services, and his mother worked as a storekeeper at a nearby cloth factory.

After nine years of marriage, medical complications, and countless prayers, Mr. and Mrs. Goel were blessed with a son. Thus, they considered his birth to be a divine blessing from Lord Krishna and named him 'Vardaan,' which means "blessing" in Hindi.

The devoted couple committed themselves to ensuring that their beloved son received the best upbringing possible. Every day, they selflessly made many sacrifices, both big and small, to give him a life full of love and endless opportunities.

Vardaan was an exceptionally bright student who brought immense pride to his family. During his Primary School years, he became widely known for his outstanding academic achievements, earning admiration from both peers and teachers alike. He was revered by students and admired by teachers for his remarkable personality, unwavering discipline, and exceptional intellectual abilities. Thus, as he progressed to senior school, Vardaan not only excelled in his studies but also took on the prestigious role of Head Prefect.

Despite facing financial challenges, Vardaan's father decided to enrol him in private tuition from seventh grade onwards. This was because his son had expressed his dream of becoming an engineer, which needed focused educational intervention. Vardaan deeply admired his parents' selfless love and, in his youthful innocence, made a silent pledge to himself to honour their sacrifices by excelling in everything he did.

Vardaan cherished the moments spent with his mother in their tiny kitchen garden. The two of them found great joy in nurturing their plants, tending to them with care, and meticulously weeding out any unwanted growth. Despite Vardaan's busy schedule filled with school, extra classes, and preparation for entrance exams, the little time spent in the garden was a precious respite for both mother and son.

Not surprisingly, Vardaan accomplished an impressive feat by clearing his Joint Entrance Examination (JEE) on his very first attempt, securing admission to the esteemed college of his dreams. The joyous occasion was marked by an outpouring of congratulations for the Goel family, who were overjoyed and showered with well-wishes.

As Vardaan made preparations to depart from home in a few days, his parents experienced a bittersweet mix of emotions. They were filled with sadness at the thought of his farewell. Yet, amidst this emotional tug, they were also incredibly happy, with an intense swell of pride and excitement for the multitude of opportunities that awaited him.

As the young boy stepped onto the sprawling campus, he was greeted by the sight of acres of verdant greenery. The esteemed faculty of the college was renowned for their knowledge and expertise. The college also boasted a wide array of curricular, co-curricular, and extra-curricular activities, all aimed at fostering the holistic development and welfare of its students.

Friends and family told him that only the journey to the campus was testing and that his career was going to run on autopilot from there. However, reality was something else. For most of Vardaan's life, he had been the forerunner in the class, but now he found himself surrounded by the top students from all over the country, creating a whole new level of competition.

Vardaan was incredibly fixated on maintaining a flawless academic record, obsessing over achieving nothing less than A grades, which put immense pressure on him. Even though the university provided an array of cultural clubs and entertaining competitions aimed at fostering a sense of community, Vardaan seemed disinterested in things beyond his academic performance, ultimately leading to the loss of his once lively and engaging personality.

The first time he returned home, his mother noticed a marked change in her son. She was expecting Vardaan to relax in her lap and indulge in his favourite meals, gardening and lively conversations. Instead, she observed a palpable air of anxiety and stress surrounding Vardaan. She couldn't help but wonder if someone at college was causing him distress, not realising that his greatest challenge was the weight of his own expectations.

Throughout his years on campus, Vardaan was unaware that he was grappling with an obsessive-compulsive disorder (OCD) commonly known as Studyholism, which is an intense obsession with studying. This obsession with academics permeated every aspect of his life, encroaching on his bedtime, meal breaks, college events and festivals. He always felt a relentless compulsion to dedicate himself to his studies, and this overwhelming sense of responsibility for his academic performance led to symptoms of depression, frequent headaches, digestive problems, and disrupted sleep patterns.

As time went on, his productivity and efficiency declined, and he struggled to focus on his assignments. As a result, it took him twice as long to complete tasks. By the last semester, while his peers were preparing to graduate with cherished memories and experiences of life on campus, Vardaan had minimal social involvement.

Finally, after countless hours of hard work, Vardaan graduated with a commendable score. Though he still considered his performance below his expectations, he was placed above the majority of his peers in class. His parents couldn't help but shed tears of joy as Vardaan handed them his well-earned graduation certificate.

To add to their happiness, their son had already secured a prestigious job at a leading IT company in Bangalore. They were thrilled to note that his annual starting salary package exceeded their combined earnings of the past five years!

The ageing Mr and Mrs Goel decided to relocate to live with their son. They were now settled in a spacious and well-appointed ground-floor apartment with three bedrooms. Their home had many modern appliances, and mundane tasks such as grinding spices, washing utensils, and washing clothes became effortless. With an intent to keep any discomfort at bay, Vardaan also employed two domestic helpers who took care of cooking and cleaning.

Despite the modern comforts and conveniences that this new way of life provided, the couple couldn't help but observe that their beloved Vardaan seldom displayed a hearty laugh or even a sincere smile.

At work, just like school and college, Vardaan thrived on exceeding expectations. He constantly pushed himself to meet tight deadlines, eagerly took on new projects, and often found himself shouldering more work than he could handle. His OCD of Studyholism had now transformed into a full-blown AD (Anxiety Disorder).

He was almost always physically exhausted, burning the candle at both ends and achieving the grand sum of zero most days in terms of his Happiness Quotient. After a very long day in the office, his only way to unwind was with a few pegs of whiskey. Sending emails in the early morning hours gave him a high, as he felt ahead of everyone else who may be still asleep.

In three years, workaholism gave Vardaan a substantial hike in both his salary and his professional profile. However, nothing satisfied him as he continued to strive for perfection. Soon, his team started to see him as a pressure vault. Their smallest flaws would trigger intense outbursts, and he frequently subjected them to emotional distress by comparing their work performance to his own.

The unchanging course of life came to a devastating halt on a balmy, humid evening when an unexpected tragedy struck. Vardaan's father, a pillar of strength and guidance in his life, succumbed to a sudden and severe heart attack, leaving Vardaan reeling in profound loss and disorientation.

This unexpected and shattering event marked the end of an era as Vardaan struggled with the immense void left by his father, a prominent figure whose influence had shaped and propelled every one of Vardaan's achievements up to that point.

Vardaan took on the sole responsibility of caring for his mother. However, the most sought-after IT networking event of the year was slated to take place six days after his father's death. "It is just a matter of a day's travel, and I can spend quality time with Maa after the event," he thought and decided to travel.

His years of experience in the Corporate world taught him to master the skill of projecting different personas to fit into various professional settings. So, despite feeling burdened, he made a conscious effort to appear cheerful, confident, and optimistic at the event. This way, he tried to conceal his inner turmoil behind an "invisible mask." But it's said that the last straw is what breaks the camel's back.

While Vardaan was in the midst of finalising a major IT project bid, his uncle called with another distressing news. Vardaan learned that his mother, Mrs. Goel, had been hospitalised due to dangerously low blood sugar levels and a nervous breakdown. This unexpected turn of events led to a sudden outpouring of shock, panic, and sorrow.

Little did he know, this day marked the beginning of an extraordinary new chapter in his life. As he worked towards his mother's recovery and dealt with the loss of his father, he found himself reflecting on the sacrifices he had made in the name of success. During this period, he came to a profound realisation about the true value of what he had been risking all along.

This experience became a turning point in his life, leading to the most important lesson he had ever learned: the importance of practising care for his loved ones and self-love.

"It was clear to him that in our lives, we must be like a flower that does not compete with the flower next to it; it just blooms! Yes, his over-competitiveness originated to honour his parents' sacrifices and to make the family's future happy. However, he had lost the precious present, worrying about the past and future."

Vardaan also began to recognise the mental and physical warning signals he had been disregarding for so long. Upon this realisation, he went through stages of anger, denial, and eventually acceptance, and now he desired to rise like a phoenix.

A few days later, he walked out of a well-known psychotherapist's room with a prescription for anti-depressants, a sick note confirming a mental breakdown and a hope that, like other ailments, his condition was totally curable.

The therapist began by candidly explaining the difference between hope and expectation. He said, "If we lose hope, we feel like giving up. But if we choose hope, there could be endless possibilities. On the other hand, when there is expectation, disappointment is almost always inevitable."

Thus, Vardaan embarked on his first month of treatment with a motivated, gutsy determination to get better. Instead of expecting instant gratification from his treatment, Vardaan made slow yet steady progress. He started with journaling and guided meditation, avoided alcohol, and embraced a balanced diet as he proceeded.

Fast-forward five years from the start of his healing journey, Vardaan leads a fulfilling life with his mother, his wife Sonia, and their two-year-old son Som. While Sonia enjoys reading spiritual books in peace, Vardaan loves to get his hands dirty in the garden with his mother and toddler.

The gentle breeze on their cheeks, the soothing aroma of flowers, the feeling of the earth beneath their feet, and the chirping of birds in their garden give the family immense joy. Unlike in the past, now, whenever situations in the office overwhelm Vardaan, he is able to tame his racing thoughts by relaxing with his nonjudgmental green friends.

Focusing on a fulfilling task like gardening now allows even complex thoughts to flow through him without negatively impacting him. As he digs over the soil or pulls the weeds, he talks about the bliss he gets from planting and cultivating something tangible and beautiful, like flowers, vegetables, and fruits.

Vardaan is a true example of how people with a history of mental health challenges can recover and truly lead meaningful lives by manifesting self-love. He has found his antidote to stress in gardening. Have you found yours yet?

Story 8

Fully Feeling is fully healing!

Samantha Singh's earliest memory takes her back to her carefree childhood, where she enjoyed laughter, dance, melodious songs, pets, and the vastness of the ocean. She vividly recalls feeling the mud caked on her feet, the cool touch of grass, and the warmth of sand as each exciting day came to an end.

Samantha and her sister Linda spent their formative years in various port cities due to their father's service in the Navy. Growing up in places like Goa and Port Blair, Samantha developed a deep appreciation for oceanic life. While Linda dedicated herself to her studies, Samantha found solace in the sea.

After school, she frequently treated herself to leisurely swims and enjoyed relaxing walks with her mother on the pristine beaches, soaking in the awe-inspiring views of the verdant surroundings and lively marine life. The salty sea breeze, the seemingly endless expanse of water, the boundless horizon, and the captivating sapphire sky combined to create a sense of freedom, leaving Samantha with a profound connection to the ocean.

Every evening, when Dad wasn't at sea, he'd come into Samantha and Linda's room to give them a tender kiss on the forehead, tuck them in, and ensure they were comfortable, even if they were fast asleep. This loving gesture meant the world to Samantha and Linda. They equated their dad's affection with the ebb and flow of the waves, always departing but ultimately returning. His kisses were a constant reassurance of his love, even when he was away on his voyages.

Due to their Navy lifestyle, the Singh family was unconventional in their mannerisms and beliefs. Samatha's mother grew up being taught by British nuns, and thus, English was the first language at home. The cross-religion mix made their lives even more interesting, as Mrs Singh was a Catholic Christian and Mr Singh a Sikh. Both girls, however, spent more time with their mother and decided to practice Christianity.

The sister duo had a striking resemblance in their looks. However, unlike Linda, Samatha spoke less. She would rather sway with the waves and let the rhythm of the water quiet her mind. She had a fascinating quality of compassion even when she was a little girl, and pets were an important (and adorable!) part of her life. Every time she was sombre or anxious, a wagging tail or a sweet meow melted her worries away.

She truly believed that almost all living creatures can build bonds with humans and thus had loads of pets in different shapes and sizes—dogs, cats, birds, and chickens. She even considered a snake as part of their family, just because it had a burrow in their garden!

During Samantha's eleventh year, her family relocated from the quaint coastal town to Delhi's vibrant and bustling city. Leaving behind the soothing embrace of the serene ocean, which had always been her cherished confidant, and adapting to the rapid rhythm of life in the metropolis posed a significant transition for Samantha. As she endeavoured to find her place in this new setting, a whirlwind of emotions swirled within her, marking the beginning of an enthralling journey ahead.

As Samantha entered her new school in a frock and two pigtails, the kids of her age seemed too grown up and mature to her. Although she felt she was very different from them, her classmates felt a natural kinship with her and were implicitly drawn to her kind nature. Her fine academic performance, participation in sports, and love for art soon made her popular amongst teachers and students across her school.

Years passed, and Samantha made peace with the chaotic city as she finished her Intermediate.

It was Samatha's first day at Delhi University, and she felt enthusiastic about her new college life. Suddenly, the Blue Line bus stopped and also halted her racing thoughts. Her destination was just five minutes away, and she had to make it to the other end of the bus, towards the exit gate. Gradually crossing many people on the bus, most standing, she carefully approached the gate.

Suddenly, she felt a touch. Someone tapped her belly and quickly moved away. Not overthinking about it and thinking it could be accidental, she proceeded to find a filthy-looking guy standing in front of her. Despite several requests, the guy pushed her as if he didn't even see her and, before she could realise it, grabbed her thighs. Even after learning about the culprit, Samantha couldn't react as she was already at the exit, obstructing other passengers. As she left the bus, her chirpiness was gone, and she felt extremely uncomfortable, unsafe, and trembling.

The traumatising public transportation left her mentally drained. All she could think about throughout the journey was how to protect herself from being rubbed and touched. Samatha hated her strategy of dealing with this challenge: to deploy silence and meekly commute in fear. However, she still couldn't gather the courage to react, making her even more disgusted.

The daily commute also brought back the mental wounds left on her adolescent mind by a few cheap relatives and neighbours who looked at her developing body in lust.

The distance between home and college was thirty-five kilometres, and personal transport was not an option. But enough was enough, so Samantha teamed up with her class buddy Judy to go hitchhiking instead of taking the Blue Line bus.

The young ladies encountered intoxicated drivers and eve-teasers at times, but as compared to everyday physical harassment, dealing with once-in-a-while challenges during hitchhiking seemed better. Nevertheless, they played safe and ensured they travelled together and boarded cars with no more than one man. Although they spoke to their carmates, they always made sure not to discuss any personal details. They changed at least two vehicles to take a drop somewhat away from college or home.

At Delhi University, Samatha was part of AIESEC, a well-known student-driven organisation. It developed her leadership capabilities and exposed her to significant events, fests, cultural workshops, and competitions. She even worked as a Radio Jockey hosting English music during midnight hours.

After college, Samatha decided to pursue her Master's in Economics from the prestigious Delhi School of Economics. The young student felt that the mental rigour and challenges that this postgraduate program threw at her evolved her brain to be cutting-edge. She could easily make confusing or difficult decisions, and the course prepared her to face the ever-changing world more confidently.

There was much more to university life than conditioning her brain and developing the qualities of a leader. She also encountered her first few trysts with divinity but was too naïve to understand the depth of these instances at that time.

One such divine intervention was how a fruitful career opportunity unexpectedly flowed to her! Linda wanted to pursue Hotel Management and applied for a Management Trainee position at a prestigious Hotel Training Academy. She looked pristine in a well-pleated saree and a picture-perfect hair bun. Samantha knew what this interview meant to Linda and decided to drop her off at the interview venue in her Maruti 800.

Casually attired in track pants and a green baggy sweater, she hopped out of the car to hug her sibling and wish her luck. Linda looked so pretty that day, Samatha wondered. Just when she was about to leave, she recalled her nasty public transportation experiences. She imagined strangers ogling Linda and touching her inappropriately on her way back home. Disturbed by this thought, Samantha decided to wait until the selection process ended.

As she basked in the winter sun, the dean of the Training Academy saw the young, confident, dusky Samantha. He gently introduced himself and invited her to wait comfortably in the lounge. Seeing his gracious personality and demeanour, Samantha accepted the invitation and hesitatingly stepped inside. Little did she know that she would end up applying for the selection rounds (in her shabby sweater and pants) and even make it to this academy that most applicants were afraid to even dream of! Although Linda was not selected, she saw her dream come true through Samantha.

The young lass was letting life flow when she met Karan, a fair, charming boy who was a year senior to her in the academy. From ragging days to bittersweet brawls, Karan and Samantha enjoyed each other's company and fell in love.

Karan had recently graduated and accepted a position in Kolkata. Samantha, one batch junior to him, also relocated to the same city a few months later.

After a year of working together in the City of Joy, Karan surprised Samantha with a heartfelt proposal during a fun-filled Friday night with friends. Overwhelmed with excitement and deeply in love, the young couple mutually decided to take the next step to tie the knot.

The couple dreamed about a beautiful life together, but what they thought was love turned out to be only attachment. Karan had lots of friends and acquaintances and enjoyed their company. Samantha also enjoyed popularity in her personal and professional circles because of her captivating personality. This was well accepted before their marriage. However, after becoming Samantha's husband, Karan's paranoia surfaced.

While he enjoyed relaxing with friends during his time off, he couldn't shake a growing unease caused by Samantha's interactions with men, even if they were everyday exchanges.

On most occasions, he overreacted with yells and accusations in the most over-the-top manner, leaving Samantha shocked. Although he usually calmed down within a few hours of his rant and apologised, it was hard for Samantha to let go and move on, knowing that he would eventually repeat it.

Karan cared for her but inadvertently started controlling her life, and whenever she was out of sight, his own fears and insecurities about "losing" her caught on his mind. Such jealousy and anger gradually eroded trust, creating emotional turmoil and making Samantha feel more suffocated with every passing day.

She was tired of this cycle of justifying her unhappy wedlock to herself. Her marriage, which started like a complete Bollywood flick, with all flavours of ideal in-laws to a perfect man, was flipped, with part 2 of it being complete inverse. After enduring resentment, accusations, pain, and rage almost every day for four years, she finally concluded that she could not swim to new horizons until she gathered the courage to leave the shore.

She gathered courage, involved her parents and sister, and communicated her decision to leave the marriage to Karan and his family. Although Karan was devastated by her decision, Samantha was firm that a relationship devoid of love, emotional safety, happiness, trust, and peace must be ended. Finally, the divorce was concluded with mutual consent.

It was the end of September, and a mild breeze drifted off the harbour, but it seemed like a cruel joke, hinting at coolness but offering no respite. Recently divorced, she felt liberated but emotionally drained, and tears streamed down her cheeks often.

Karan and Samantha have been a famous couple since their Training Academy days, but rumours of their breakup gained even more popularity. Thus, Samantha took a transfer to Delhi to start her new life!

While packing for Delhi, she came across a few old pictures. They reminded her of the statement her dean made to her parents on Hotel Academy's graduation day. He said, "Your daughter has a spine made of steel, and she can win over any hardship in life!"

It's strange how one important person's belief can change our lives, even in our darkest times.

The dean's conviction also served as a beacon to enlighten Samantha's path and rekindled her self-belief.

Before her official joining in Delhi, the Singh family decided to take a holiday to Goa. They knew that for Samatha, salt water—sweat, tears, or the sea—was the cure for almost everything.

On the first day of this vacation, Samantha gently kept her head in her dad's lap while tears trickled down her cheeks. She expected to be coddled or encouraged to look at the bright side. But her father's reaction was different. She wasn't told to gloss over her feelings with a smile but to *feel her pain in its entirety*. Dad explained that "We cannot heal what we don't feel" and "pain is authentic and productive—a necessary step on our journey towards healing."

His direct acknowledgement of Samantha's suffering brought about further psychological strength as she understood the need to truly feel her emotions instead of avoiding them. Instead of worrying that she wasn't trying hard enough to be happy and that she may take "too long" to heal, she felt like a phoenix rising from the ashes in all her glory.

In the next few months, she gradually summoned compassion for herself while navigating through uncomfortable feelings. She soon felt herself walking on the path to healing, peace, and wholeness. We know that fire purifies everything! Samantha had also experienced fire (in the form of psychological distress) and felt cleansed and purified in the end.

It is true that when we make space in our lives by keeping self-pity at bay, the right things just fall into place. Samantha experienced this as she met her spiritual guru, who introduced her to Vipassana meditation and Kundalini awakening and gave her tips on how she could work towards closing her karmic cycle. For most people, divinity comes in the darkest phases of their lives. However, Samatha's spiritual journey started when she was already experiencing mental bliss.

Free of people's opinions and with deep self-love, Samantha zealously focussed on her career. Her work was absorbing and encompassing. She experienced great success and awful days in the corporate world, where a workgroup ganged up against her for selfish interests. However, Samantha was unstoppable! She was bolder, calmer, and had augmented confidence, which she considered a gift from God after her rough marriage.

On a personal front, although Samantha met a few good men, she did not think of rushing into a bond again. She wanted to apply the learnings from her broken marriage before jumping into a new relationship. So, her dates were very different, as she didn't try to impress a man; she only wanted to see if the direction of their lives was compatible. Samantha had stopped looking for love and was no longer afraid to be alone.

The best way to find love is to let love find you. This is precisely what Samantha experienced when she met Tejas at a school reunion. A casual coffee date after the event transitioned into daily calls and frequent meetings. Seven years after divorce, Samantha had found love!

Tejas's simplicity, zest for life, and authenticity attracted her to form a meaningful connection, which resulted in marriage after a year of courtship. Samatha has been enjoying a fulfilling marital life for the past nine years. In this imperfect life, Tejas and Samatha are like two halves of a puzzle who fit well and make each other blissfully happy by simply supporting each other through thick and thin times.

Tejas's love, however, has not been a deterrent in nurturing Samantha's self-love, which is getting deeper with guided meditation. Her voyage inwards helped her treat many psychological and even physical conditions like chronic bronchitis, spinal aches, and migraines. People who meet her often compliment her as they feel she is ageing in reverse at 47 years!

Samantha has a powerful message for all who are reading her story: "When you start putting yourself first, love from the universe flows to you. My self-love manifested amazingly, as I am blessed with a partner who lives joyfully and fearlessly through life's challenges. I feel privileged today to be surrounded by a loving ecosystem put together by the universe."

Our lives as humans are flawed! It is our natural tendency to search for means to avoid our scars and numb our agony. I wanted to showcase Samantha's life as she continues to use pain as a gateway to a fuller life and lives by the mantra “Fully feeling is fully healing”!

Afterword

Discovering your passion and combining it with your purpose and natural talents is a guaranteed way to create a powerful legacy. I have found my true calling in writing, and I am driven by an unwavering desire to leave a meaningful legacy through my books.

As a result, this anthology has been created with a lot of time, effort, and genuine emotions. It would mean a lot to me if any of these real-life anecdotes could inspire, encourage, and uplift the spirits of the readers.

Acknowledgements

Following the resounding success of my debut book, "I'm in Love with Me", I was inspired to dream bigger. I am indebted to **all the readers who not only embraced my work but also** shared their honest feedback, heartfelt encouragement, and reviews. Your support has been instrumental in keeping my spirits alive.

Listening to stories, turning them into a manuscript and finally sewing them together in a book is harder than it sounds. But the experience is both eternally tough and rewarding.

I especially want to thank my awesome husband **Punit**, our adorable daughter **Ourjaa** and nephew **Saksham,** who were by my side throughout this journey. From reading early drafts to giving me advice on the cover page, their contribution was substantial.

My father, **Kameshwar Nath,** mother-in-law**,** **Snehlata** and son, **Tanishque,** adore me as their shero, and the pride in their eyes strengthens me to soar higher.

Maa's blessings, I know, are always with me as I walk on the stimulating trail called life!

Most importantly, my heartfelt gratitude goes to **all those who graciously allowed me to feature their stories in my book**. Your trust and contribution have truly transformed the trajectory of my life. Without you, this book would not have been possible.

www.ingramcontent.com/pod-product-compliance
Ingram Content Group UK Ltd.
Pitfield, Milton Keynes, MK11 3LW, UK
UKHW062254290726
14090UKWH00017B/675